ENUMERATOR

AN IRREVERENT MEMOIR

ANNALEE F. COBBETT

For my parents, Karen and Bob

Nothing is more wonderful than the art of being free, but nothing is harder to learn how to use than freedom.

—Alexis de Tocqueville

TABLE OF CONTENTS

THE GREAT RECESSION

A poor lawyer I was. Freshly shorn of my law practice like a bad haircut, I arrived in California on Labor Day 2008 as the Great Recession leveled the U.S. economy. Even with my law degree, I struggled to find work in the Golden State; Office Manager and like positions I got for a time by bowdlerizing my resume to omit my J.D. and fifteen years' experience practicing law.

My first few months in Oakland, across the Bay from San Francisco, I scored good-paying temporary gigs doing document review at a handful of large San Francisco law firms. Those of us who did this sort of work were treated like second-class hacks who couldn't make it in the big leagues. We got the cold shoulder in the hallway from the senior partners; even the junior associates snubbed us. I was

1

there for the money and had already made up my mind to leave law, clicking through an endless stream of discovery documents, analyzing them for relevance, privilege, and work product. Next, next, next. Eight or nine hours sitting before a computer screen aggravated my concern about what work I, a single, 45-year-old lesbian woman, could get when the current project ended.

As a licensed attorney, I was trained to solve other people's problems, but when the doc review jobs dried up, I found myself relying on food stamps and unemployment for nearly two years. Mocked by my former lawyer status, I was on the public dole, and worse, I couldn't see a way out. It wasn't for lack of trying that I couldn't find work—countless Americans were in the same boat as me.

Hundreds of us gathered at networking meetups, desperate for job leads, and sat through yet another PowerPoint presentation about using LinkedIn to beg for work from those clinging tooth-and-toenail to their own jobs. The forced idleness of unemployment caused my depression to resurface. On "the beach," the driveway of my apartment complex, I laid in the warm sun to melt the brain fog. I'd seemingly fallen into someone else's reality, and a midlife crisis bloomed like algae on a stagnant lake.

Over the fall and winter of 2009, I broke through frozen fear every morning like an Arctic icebreaker to ramp up my job search. My dread was losing my apartment and having to find housing with my tabby cat, Austin and no job. More than once I considered pulling the pin, and my howls of frustration were drowned out by the horn blasts of hurtling locomotives passing below the pedestrian bridge.

At the end of January, on a whim, I attended the 2010 U.S. Census kickoff event in downtown Oakland. Mayor Dellums spoke about the importance of an accurate census count, and I waited until the end for free coffee, cake, and a 2010 Census tote bag—unbeknownst to me, the first of several I'd own. A jazz quartet played in the town square, and a moment of goodwill descended upon me in the sparse crowd. I took a deep breath and looked around, smiling at everyone eating cake, and the sun peeped out after two weeks of rain.

Oakland, California, the second-most diverse city its size in the U.S. has a high homeless population, where housing costs rival those of New York City, but the weather is generally so fine one needs no house to live. Its crime ranks Oakland as one of America's most dangerous cities; 9-1-1 makes you hold for twenty minutes when you call, and you're lucky if the police show up.

A war zone, I walked around fearing shooting and mugging. Growing resentment between the rich and poor, crooked cops, and a history of protests in nearby Berkeley ignited the town's incendiary racial politics, utterly foreign to my sheltered suburban upbringing. For perhaps the first time since moving here the census event made me feel Oakland united in community.

I forgot about my application for the census-taker job and was surprised in February when they invited me to take the Enumerator exam. In normal times, I wouldn't bother, but with the recession underway, I took the exam in a basement conference room with hundreds of other candidates. The test wasn't difficult: basic math and organization skills.

In March, the census job came through—my test score had been sufficient—but I was leery. In which neighborhood would I work, and how would I get there? Would I be safe? I didn't relish slogging down rain-soaked streets, chased by dogs, and Tea Partiers raving in my face about the Second Amendment. I prayed that one of my other job applications would come through.

The job intimidated me, and I made fun of the census in a blog post. I didn't want to go door-to-door and ask people questions, yet $22 an hour was a port in the recession storm. Like most people, I'd never devoted a single thought to the U.S. Census and couldn't care less about it. Hoping something better would turn up before the training started, I accepted the census job.

NRFU

My first day of paid census training arrived in mid-April 2010, and the regimented instruction after my long period of unemployment made me feel like a rookie Army recruit. The trainers read from scripts four hours each day of the training week. Seizing the opportunity to blog about my census experience "from the inside," I scribbled notes to spice up my blog posts from my ringside seat.

Other than my cat, my Wordpress blog gave me more pleasure than anything else. I began blogging in September 2009, one year to the day after moving to California, with humorous commentary on news and culture from a feminist viewpoint. Three times a week I posted entries, and it gave me a reason to get up in the morning. I'd gained a number of blog followers, and my writing was improving before an appreciative audience—one of the few lights on my dim horizon.

Fellow trainees, seated in neat rows, hailed from all walks of life: dreadlocked, retired, parents, geeks—the formerly unemployed of all stripes. I felt trapped, out of place, yet relieved to have something constructive to do and, if I was honest, to be amongst other humans instead of alone.

Odessa, our middle-aged Black trainer, stood at the front of the room and droned monotonously into the mic, "If you do not complete a D-1199, then you must complete a D-260." Government forms, publications, and pamphlets are all numbered, and we learned to refer to them by number and acronym. Everyone looked sleepy and bored, and someone propped open the training room door, admitting a welcome spring breeze that kept me from dozing off.

Jarring me from stupor, the trainer said, "If you don't fill in the racial info on the D-168, I will fill it in for you based on my observations of you." Suddenly, the unbidden specter of race entered the room, and we shifted nervously in our seats and glanced sidelong at the rainbow of skin colors filling the seats. Little did we know this was just the tip of the racial iceberg that would rear its head on our new job.

Trainers plowed the trainees through filling out federal employment forms en masse. Then we—old and young, women and men—collectively stood and raised our right hands as bidden by the trainer.

We pledged allegiance to the United States Constitution and swore to uphold the government and defend it from all enemies, foreign and domestic.

The census is a national "selfie" about who we are, what we look like, where we live and sleep—and with whom. We learned that Article 1, Section 2 of the United States Constitution requires the government to count the U.S. population every ten years. As a census enumerator, it was my job to follow up and visit those who didn't fill out and mail back the questionnaire to ensure that every last resident was counted.

August 2, 1790, marked the first American census, when Secretary of State Thomas Jefferson sent U.S. Marshals on horseback to count dwellers. Only six questions made up the first census, including the name of the white male householder and his slaves, who counted as three-fifths of a person until the Fourteenth Amendment was ratified in 1868. That I discovered later, since it wasn't mentioned in the training.

During a stern lecture about federal law protecting census data from disclosure, I first heard the acronym PII—Personally Identifiable Information—which could be used to identify an individual, such as name, address, or social security number. Each Census Bureau employee takes a lifetime oath to keep PII confidential. By law, the respondents' PII is protected from disclosure for 72 years.

The importance of PII was driven home by the blue cover of our D-590 Census Employee Handbook, with a drawing of a keyhole in the back of a person's head, representing the lifetime confidentiality oath. They took everyone's fingerprints twice, and I felt the seriousness of my responsibility to protect respondents' personal information the same way I would want mine guarded from disclosure.

During fingerprinting, the technician grabbed each of my hands to ink the fingers and press them into boxes printed on the paper. We all watched each other get fingerprinted, and some of the older trainees acted like no human being had touched them in years, making me feel that others had been more isolated than me in these difficult days.

I felt lost in the cattle drive atmosphere, demeaned by the bureaucratic numbered forms, the jargon; it made me feel insignificant. *Welcome back to the Wonderful World of Work*, I thought—*and, particularly, employment in a government agency.* The trainers moved me around and told me where to stand, and it triggered memories of past unpleasant job experiences and abusive bosses. A hungry feeling, an emotional neediness, tugged at my gut, and the question arose: is all this effort worth it for a few weeks' work?

My angst was momentarily overcome by excitement when they issued each of us a black canvas shoulder bag loaded with manuals and supplies. In white writing it displayed the Census 2010 logo and the slogan, "Helping You Make Informed Decisions." I explored the "Kit G-6, Field Trainee, Paper Operations Only" contents:

No. 2 Pencil, 4 each
Pencil Sharpener, Plastic, 1 each
Pencil Eraser, 4 each
Ballpoint Pen, Blue, 2 each
Paper Clips, 1 box

Swirling a No. 2 pencil in the plastic sharpener, I noted the low-tech nature of the data collection. While unsophisticated, the secure, time-tested and cost-effective pencil-and-paper method had served the census well since its beginning. Despite the internet being well-established by 2010, its potential for census data collection was passed over in favor of traditional hand-completed forms. In many ways, the 2010 Census was conducted as if the internet didn't yet exist, forcing a belated rearguard action by the Bureau to tamp down online gossip and criticism.

Training week flew by, and I prepared to conduct my first interview. With the census bag slung over my shoulder like a rifle, I was ready for anything the American public could throw at me. It was difficult to imagine myself out there toting around people's Personally Identifiable Information—and I wasn't sure I could manage even with the comprehensive training, but I was game to try.

LIVE AND SLEEP

On the last morning of training, Odessa explained, "We keep pestering them until we get the interview." As emphasized during training, we count people "where they live and sleep most of the time" – this was central to our mission. One enumerator, and then another, would visit the respondents until we breached their defenses. We wouldn't leave until we found out the number of persons in each home and whether it was vacant, seasonal, rental, or vacation. She said, "Don't ask, 'May I come back?' Ask, '*When* may I come back?'" Ten minutes and ten questions are all we need, and we counted day after day in army-ant formation until we tallied everyone.

Nonresponse Followup, or NRFU, is when census enumerators go door-to-door to personally administer the questionnaire to the approximately one-quarter of households that didn't fill it out and return it by early April. It's critical to get the respondent interview and data for an accurate count, and enumerators are trained to be creative and persistent to obtain this vital information.

During NRFU, those residents who didn't return their completed questionnaire can expect a visit from an enumerator. Like Mary and Joseph returning to Bethlehem to pay taxes, census participation is not optional. These holdouts' PII was on a spreadsheet inside my census shoulder bag, and I was heading their way.

Since the following day was my first day of enumerating, that evening I pored over the D-547 Manual section, "Handling Refusals and Reluctant Respondents." My biggest worry was unruly responders, and the Manual suggested canned answers to handle possible protests.

If the resident says, "I don't have time," the enumerator can say the census questionnaire only takes a few minutes to complete.

If they say, "That is none of your business," I can respond, "Everyone's participation is vital, and each question helps Congress make decisions."

To the statement, "You are wasting my time and money," I was to tell them the census determines each state's representation in the U.S. House of Representatives.

3. LIVE AND SLEEP

If the person was a non-English speaker, our D-590 manual instructed us to find a household member who spoke English to interpret. If no English speaker was available, "Hold up the D-3309 Language Identification Flashcard and motion for the respondent to point to the language he or she speaks," be it Farsi, Tagalog, or Russian. The Census Bureau would later send the appropriate interpreter to record their answers.

Places without postal delivery are enumerated in person: Toksook Bay, Alaska, traditionally the first community to be counted in the census, was counted first as in previous years. The ceremonial kickoff was in January when the ground was frozen, allowing access to fishing villages via snowmobile and dogsled.

RESPONDENTS

In the morning I strode out to uphold my Constitutional oath, and completed two Enumerator Questionnaires (EQs) on my first day. My assigned neighborhood, only blocks from my own, basked in the spring sunshine. With my plastic white government identification badge centered on its lanyard between my breasts, and the black census shoulder bag, I knocked and rang and mostly found nobody home. After the interviews, I completed the paperwork on someone's shady front step among the ants, whose work I now identified with.

Census data determines the share of federal tax money for each state and local government, including funding for schools, law enforcement, roads, and Medicare. Over 300 federal spending programs use census data to divide funds among the states. Nationwide, the census count governs the distribution of $1.5 trillion per year of federal dollars.

Walking two blocks home after a successful pair of interviews, a Paul McCartney song played in my head: "We're so sorry, Uncle Albert, we haven't done a bloody thing all day." Counting people like sheep, where they live and sleep, seemed pretty easy so far.

Before long, I identified several types of respondents on my rounds.

Busybodies

Like a dog when its owner picks up the leash, some residents fell all over themselves to provide information; they went out of their way to collar me and disgorge information about their neighbors, who got shot where, and which houses burned down. Thanks to them, I got the EQ answers for vacant apartments and people who didn't answer the door.

Likely Stories

The actual excuses I heard from some noncooperative respondents were so rich, I wrote them down in my notes.

I sent it in already.

I'm taking my dog to the vet now.

I have to jump in the shower.

Just leave the form and we'll mail it in.

Here's my form [still in its unopened envelope].

I can't tell you my roommate's name, we don't know if he's coming back.

Talk to my girlfriend, I'm moving out.

Avoidant

A red flash exited from the side door of the home that didn't answer the doorbell, darted to her car, and peeled off. The elusive ones played a cat-and-mouse game, enjoying the pursuit. "Foiled again," they seemed to cry as they decamped, leaving me in the dust. Avoidants seized the chance to play "outwit the enumerator." Their car was parked in the driveway, but the house remained quiet as a church—too silent to be empty.

Why they needed to avoid the U.S. Census Bureau, I never knew, but some introverts deal best with computers.

Deep Cover

Most reclusive were those who, no matter what, didn't open the door. They seemed to feel no good could come of it and remained deep in hiding. My heart sank each time I mounted their steps, rang, or knocked. I heard children's pounding feet or faint television but knew from previous experience the door would not open for me. I stood helplessly and felt myself being watched from behind dingy blinds.

HAZARDS

Turned out my concerns about safety on the job were well-founded: out of 635,000 enumerators hired by the Bureau, NRFU in its first week racked up seven enumerator deaths, six of whom perished in car accidents. The body count seemed awfully high, considering that 13 people died in car accidents during the whole 2000 Census, plus one killed by a pack of dogs.

By June 23, 2010, there had been 24 animal attacks on census workers reported, along with 132 reports of guns drawn or threatened, and 13 reports of shots fired. Also 409 threats or assaults had been made on census workers, more than double the 181 incidents during the 2000 Census. I heard through the census grapevine about two Oakland enumerators who were assaulted.

The seventh victim was the strange and well publicized case of William E. Sparkman, Jr., who was found hanging naked from a tree in eastern Kentucky with the word "FED" scrawled on his chest upside down. While the Department of Homeland Security had warned of antigovernment "jack-booted thug"-type militia activity during the census, the Bureau had never dealt with a potential murder before.

The training manual advised, "Don't defend yourself or the government with respondents who say they hate you and all government employees. Indicate that you regret this opinion and express a desire to provide them with a positive experience." The FBI determined Mr. Sparkman wrote the word "FED" on himself, trying to pin his death on the census worker, and his death was later ruled a suicide.

Safety had many angles on the job, like standing on a wood porch feeling rotten boards flex underfoot. The D-590 Handbook said, "Avoid walking on uneven, broken, or poorly constructed surfaces or stairs."

The manual had this to say about dogs:

> *Learn to recognize the warning signs that a dog is about to attack: tail high and stiff, ears up, hair on back standing up, and teeth showing. If the dog does bite you, do not pull away. It will cause a tear and a worse wound. Instead, try to make the*

dog release its hold. Here is the manual's take on "Safety When Walking Alone":

Do not carry valuables, large sums of money, expensive jewelry, and watches. As you approach your vehicle, scan beneath it for persons waiting to charge out at your ankles. Wear comfortable walking shoes. These shoes may come in handy should there be the need to run.

Run from whom or what, I wondered.

I never expected to see abandoned homes and must have walked past the dilapidated Victorian before, but never noticed it until its EQ appeared in my binder. It had chain link fence, boarded-up windows, and weeds choking the yard. A neighbor told me the back of the house was removed, open to the elements. "I don't know why they did that," she added, adding to the air of mystery about the place.

A Black man pulled his battered pickup truck over and beckoned to me. Hesitating because he was a stranger, yet curious to learn any info he might give me, I hiked up the shoulder bag and sauntered over. He called, "Hey, that house empty, nobody living there. The old man died and nobody lived there since." With a private sigh of relief—Uncle Sam trained me to handle this—the old man gave me a proxy interview for the empty residence, providing information to report the vacant house on the EQ.

Census interviews occurred almost anywhere—on a porch, sidewalk, even in a car's passenger seat, engine off and door open. Odessa, our trainer, had told us she wouldn't enter a residence, but the rules didn't forbid it. Occasionally, I accepted a resident's invitation to enter if it felt safe—usually if she were female and seemed nice.

One of my growing number of census blog post readers passed along this anecdote about a Crew Leader's warning to his enumerator team:

> *There was another mountain lion sighting near the 500 block of Helen Drive. If your AA (Assigned Area) includes this area, make sure that you are especially vigilant, particularly around dusk.*

Enumerators even had to worry about wild predators, with our closest thing to a weapon being a sharpened No. 2 pencil.

Although I carried a primitive smartphone device, few homes had outdoor surveillance cameras in 2010; at most, a few homeowners had installed security alarms on windows and doors. That all changed by the time the 2020 Census rolled around ten years later.

SELLING IT

Quickly I learned enumerating success depended on buttering up whoever answered the door, in order to get them to complete a questionnaire. When people told me they didn't have time or had already turned in their form, my game plan shifted into high gear. Half first-grade teacher and half parole officer, I implored, "If we get this done now, someone won't come back." Humility, persistence—and veiled threats—won the day almost every time.

With practice, I got the hang of persuasion and humor to pry information from the respondent gently yet firmly, sometimes racing through the EQ, the door easing slowly shut as they spoke, insisting each question would be their last… but I popped just one… more… in edgewise.

My personal rule became, "Nobody shuts the door on me while I'm talking." I'd juggle six balls while singing the National Anthem, so long as they didn't lock me out mid-sentence. It began to feel like a sales presentation: I was Willie Loman from *Death of a Salesman*. I giggled, stopped giggling, quizzically tilted my head like a cockatiel, pretended to mess up, really did mess up, corrected my mistake, and made a self-deprecating joke—anything to keep their attention on me and the form.

I imagined the person thinking, "What is the crazy census wench gonna do next?" I tried everything except pulling a white rabbit out of my shoulder bag to keep them focused on me and answering the questions.

Writers are supposedly introverts, but when the door swung open, the vaudeville performer awoke inside of me as if spotlighted on a stage. The footlights came up and I became Phyllis Diller on speed; I was "on," and shocked myself with the lengths I would go to get information out of people, all dignity out the window. But it was the most fun I'd had in a long time. I had zero to lose, and the challenge to be surmounted gave me something to strive for besides avoiding eviction.

The ominous cloud of financial anxiety lifted a little as the paychecks came in. I forgot about my problems, poked my head out of the cave to perform service to my fellow humans, and even had some laughs. A new sense of purpose drew me out of bed in the morning, the day's map and strategy already filling my head for the route I would take for the AA (assigned area).

It became a game: first, stop the door from slamming, engage the person, then housemates led me to roommates, and neighbors gushed about neighbors. Scouring the block, changing course on a dime, dashing for a neighbor exiting her vehicle, and pumping her for information, pushiness wrapped in a smiling glitter bomb.

A woman said I was brave to do this job. Nah, just ballsy and inquisitive. The reckless, feckless euphoria, an adrenaline high floating up a stranger's stairs, interrupting their dinner, demanding all the info I could. My power was borrowed yet real, an exercise in improvisation and the iron fist of government wrapped in the irresistible humanity of a real person knocking at your door.

I took to wearing an unusual, inexpensive, out-of-style necklace on my rounds, which revealed my age (over forty), lifestyle (creative), and might arouse someone's curiosity enough to open the door and answer the EQ. Silently, it communicated to them: "Before you slam the door in her face, before you stands a middle-aged woman of substance with her own unique style and goofy, winning smile, balancing the questionnaire on a black binder."

Meanwhile on the national level the Bureau outdid itself to promote Census 2010, with its own blog, a road show, and even a race car.

The No. 16 carried a special paint job in NASCAR races, with the census logo and "Mail it Back!" emblazoned on the hood. Apparently, the racer was a metaphor for the swiftness of the new census form: only 10 questions in 10 minutes.

Census Director Robert Groves said, "NASCAR racing is an effective avenue to reach a huge number of fans, reminding them their 2010 Census form will be arriving in March and to mail them back." The paid NASCAR sponsorship was practical, he said, because "for every 1 percent increase in mail response, taxpayers will save an estimated $85 million" that would otherwise be spent on NRFU workers, like me, to follow up with households that didn't "mail it back."

The Census Road Tour set out from Times Square on January 4, 2010, on a nationwide voyage to provide a "cross-country interactive experience designed to increase awareness and encourage participation in the census." Each of the 13 truck-trailer combos making up the Road Tour had a unique name and matching Twitter handle, with names like "Liberty," "Constitution," "Democracy," and "Founders," along with "Take 10," "Mail It Back," "Statistics," and the obtuse "Abacus." During its four-month journey, the Road Tour exhibited at 800 events from The Superbowl and NCAA Final Four to local parades and festivals.

The Road Tour's blog posts however, displayed a glaring absence of reader comments. Between NASCAR and the truck fleet, the Census Bureau tried to shed its green-eyeshade image for macho wheels and the compliance of beer-swilling race fans. I never did learn whether those expenditures—$1.2 million for NASCAR alone—achieved their outreach goals and justified the taxpayer investment.

NANCY DREW

Each census block was a puzzle to be solved, and my census badge gave me license to problem-solve any way I could. If Apartment D was on the list, I explored the property to find it, becoming more emboldened the more I skulked about. A crash course in navigating the neighborhood, I sniffed out vacant and hidden units, the 1/2s and basement apartments. If I needed to know when the residents of Apartment C were home, I didn't hesitate to knock on Apartment B's door, since any intel was better than none.

The detective aspect meant solving the live and sleep riddle: does anyone live up there/in that/down there? Are people out of town if a week's worth of newspapers piled up on the porch? Is Unit A upstairs or under the stairs? Do I feel safe going back there/behind the fence/in the gate? Is music coming from this house or next door? Stop, look, listen and use caution when crossing the street. The skills were basic, but their application to enumerating was a new experience.

Inside the safety cone conferred by my badge and shoulder bag, I performed feats like opening people's gates, exploring private hallways, and peering into backyards. I liberally interpreted my government flunky job as permission to do paperwork on people's steps. One afternoon, I walked into a hotel, flashed my badge at the desk clerk and said, "I'm a census worker. Can I use the bathroom?" He waved me inside like a celebrity.

Mumbling to myself like Inspector Clouseau, I checked on my Enumerator Questionnaires (EQs) safe in their manila envelope, and the wind ruffled the pages of my binder. Sometimes a paper blew away and I chased it down, keen not to lose any PII, as I'd been drilled in training. We were getting paid to follow prescribed procedures, not innovate, but there was still room for creativity.

I turned in my second completed AA binder to Matt, my CLA (Crew Leader Assistant), whom I saw daily. Matt was a bearded 24-year-old medic and mathematician, and our talk drifted, after he reviewed my forms, to conversation about facial hair. We discussed Sarah Palin's facial hair, which had been in the news, and I'd already blogged about Palin's infamous legs, also covered by the news media.

Every day, Matt asked me, "Is this EQ an in-mover?" I answered no, I'd never had an in-mover. In fact, I dreaded getting an in-mover, a resident who'd moved into the address after Census Day, April 1. First, you asked the resident if they knew who lived in the home on April 1. Then you interviewed them as if you were standing on the doorstep of the place where they lived on April 1. Confusing. Census Day, the date on which the population count is referenced, has been proposed to be a national holiday.

The process isn't perfect, and even the Bureau makes errors. I had my first "apartment mix-up" (the official government term); they switched the apartment that returned the census form with one that hadn't. A two-apartment mix-up was a simple fix; just interview whichever respondent didn't complete the EQ. The D-547 Manual discussed multiple mix-ups in apartment buildings or trailer parks: "It may be necessary to complete the correction process more than once to get an interview for a unit where you cannot find the respondent's name."

I picked a quiet doorstep to write notes and complete the EQs. The same "outdoor offices" sheltered me each time I returned to the neighborhood, and I got info from residents walking their dogs past me on the sidewalk. When I said, "Hello," while seated next to my official shoulder bag, they sometimes stopped and offered valuable insight on when and where I could locate an elusive neighbor.

Neighbors wanted to know about neighbors. There was a bottomless well of interest about one's own neck of the woods. They asked me if so-and-so returned their census form, which I couldn't reveal because it's PII. Neighbors know a lot about each other, more than they think they do. In proxy interviews they'd say, "She was Dominican. Her sister stayed with her sometimes, and she took in boarders."

A woman stood before me in the doorway wearing rubber gloves, holding a toilet brush, discussing the townhouse across the way and accenting her words with shakes of the brush. "We're a garage community," she said. "The only time I see my neighbors is when we drive in and out of the garage." People don't know their neighbors the way they used to, making it harder to get proxy info, but some people know a scary amount about their neighbors.

Another respondent answered a door holding a sagging paper plate of greasy pizza, which made my stomach rumble, and inquired about "impostor" census workers. I told her to call the census office. People would say, "What an awful job you have," and "I hear nobody's giving you any information." It wasn't true. People snitched on their neighbors constantly, and I found myself politely correcting their misconceptions.

One evening, I was out later than intended. It was dark, but it was my last chance to try the respondents in this particular neighborhood before my AA binder was assigned to another census worker. I knocked on an apartment door with a TV blaring inside. Suddenly, it got deathly quiet, but nobody answered. After a month of doing this, it was easy to tell when someone was home or not; the "quick, turn-down-the-TV" trick didn't fool me anymore.

Another EQ was for a ground-floor apartment that looked the same every time I passed, with a balled-up white cloth on the front walk. No answer for me, nor the enumerator who had the binder before me. Next door, where at least three people lived, I had the name Marilyn and a phone number given to me by the previous enumerator. Marilyn was impossible to get a hold of, and everyone who lived there seemed to be hiding in plain sight. It grew creepily quiet each time I knocked, as if the occupants were waiting for me to give up and go away—which eventually I did, making them another enumerator's problem.

Others were hungry for interaction and often drew me into animated conversation, while I tried to avoid drowning in someone's loneliness, or reached common ground with a stranger. Some conversations could have gone on for hours, but I excused myself and kept moving down the block.

All that Americans share, despite differences in wealth, faith, and skin color, stuck with me on my rounds. To these people, I was a person—not poor or unemployed or depressed, but a government peon doing my job, and they respected me for it. I began to feel the pins-and-needles awareness of the phantom limb that was work returning to my consciousness. I wasn't a nonentity collecting food stamps, but a person whose efforts made a difference in collecting vital census data while serving my country.

BLOCK ANGEL

My next AA of EQs was harder to complete because I couldn't get close enough to the residents to get interviews. The security fences were too high, I couldn't ring without a bell, and shouting wasn't an option. The freeway roared nearby, and crime was rampant in my newly assigned slice of East Oakland. My ingenuity was called upon once again.

Often one person, whom I dubbed the "block angel," was key to unlocking a whole building, or even the whole block. Enlist the lead person to my cause and the entire block came around and obediently answered the questionnaires. It behooved me to be seen chatting with the neighborhood gatekeeper, who spied me poking around and made me aware of their scrutiny. Get in good with the watchdog who had their nose in everyone's business, and it green-lighted other interviews nearby.

A middle-aged African American woman challenged me from her balcony as I warily circled the public housing complex. "Hey you, government worker!" she yelled. "Get out of here!" Ignoring my instincts, I stepped closer, steadying my nerves and smiling, feeling she was testing my resolve. As I approached, she laughed and said, "I'm only playing with you. I wouldn't do nothin'." I showed her my badge and recited my census rap like a boss. She told me, "The residents can see you, but you can't see them." After our talk, the other building denizens lined up to answer the EQs. The block angel had told them I was legit and they could trust me.

With no luck on the next block, I migrated to the opposite end of the street. Same problem: tall fences, no doorbells, no signs of life. It irked me to be unable to get close enough to knock or catch someone's attention.

One technique was to hang around until someone took pity on me and struck up a conversation. I leaned on a fence, surveying the corner like a local, and tried not to be mistaken for a prostitute— albeit one with a government badge.

The place seemed deserted in the slanted afternoon light as I hailed a sullen gaggle of males smoking on a front porch. They didn't respond to my greeting, but salvation arrived in the form of a gregarious Black man in a dented white van. He pulled in, walked over, and I felt my smile coming out like the sun from behind a cloud. Here came my key to the inaccessible block.

Sure enough, Frank turned out to be the block angel who gave me enough information to complete three questionnaires. He didn't know anything about the other end of the block, but my day's work was half done after speaking with him.

The census brought me out of a shell I didn't know I was in. When I needed something, I found out I could ask the nearest person, no matter their skin color, which ordinarily might have intimidated me. Lost in an unfamiliar neighborhood, I asked yet another older Black man—they were often the most helpful—which way was Grande Vista Street. He pointed the way with his cane like Fred Astaire, and chatted me up about how good walking is for your health. After the first week of NRFU, I knew that anyone could help, if approached in the right way.

The block angel effect faded, though, as neighbors on both sides of the freeway refused to talk, so I was off to interrogate their landlords and the "easier" street I had saved for last. The puzzle on the nicer block was a variation of the first: how to obtain interviews in high-security places. After my third fruitless visit to an apartment building, it was faster to take the EQs straight to the landlord, if I could find them, and gather all the information at once: family members, phone numbers, and move-in dates.

WHITE WOMAN

At first, I worried my being white worked against me with respondents of color. But I soon noted a white person at the door was a novelty that aroused curiosity. "Honey, there's a *white woman* at the door." Bewildered excitement was often the mood when I showed up on the doorsteps of diverse neighborhoods.

A pastry-flour white suburb of Rochester, New York, was where I grew up, and I didn't have Black, Asian, or Latino playmates. Only one Black student attended my public elementary school in the early 1970s. A Chinese family moved in, and the kids attended my school, but I didn't socialize with the few token minority families nearby. My classmates were Polish, Italian, Dutch, and Jewish—in other words, white kids.

Approaching a door and ringing the bell made me visible: a long pause, shifting foot to foot, while unseen residents sized me up. I allowed myself to be vulnerable, dropped any pretense of privilege, and caught a glimpse of a rustled curtain or falling blind slat. My small, glasses-wearing frame was imbued with the ill-fitting aura of government authority like an oversized trench coat. Their first impression determined whether they would swing the door open or hide in the depths of the dim fish tank they called home.

What did they see when this enumerator hove into view? A short, curly-haired, slightly overweight woman of indeterminate middle age. My posture, the tilt of my head, my clothing, even my shoes were open to interpretation. I held an attitude of bemused meekness, eyes downcast while I fiddled with my necklace or badge, conveying nonthreatening-ness. Always in the back of my mind was the timeworn sales technique of piquing the respondent's curiosity.

Sometimes the race barrier couldn't be overcome. Standing on a Black woman's front steps, keenly aware of our different skin colors, I asked her about the Black women across the street who never answered their door. She refused to divulge anything, and invited me to leave her property posthaste.

The census tries to capture reality and diversity in statistics, and enumerators themselves are Black, White, Asian, Latino, every race and culture. But enumerators were matched to their assigned neighborhoods geographically, not by race—no Black enumerator showing up on every African American doorstep. Neither life nor the census is that tidy.

Each day, the California enumerators dealt with dozens of races and a plethora of languages. The census reflected the experience of having someone of another race come to your door to count you. My newfound appreciation for multiculturalism, like the grain of sand in the machinery, encouraged me to work harder to communicate with respondents who didn't look like me. Without second-guessing, I wrote down whatever race the person claimed to be, or as one woman said, "Just white."

There were hiccups over race, like the argument I witnessed between the Bosnian guy and his Salvadoran wife about whether he was white. Census race questions are written awkwardly enough to suggest a backroom political compromise over their wording. On the volatile subject of ethnicity, the U.S. Census Bureau wasn't immune from racial controversy affecting the culture at large, which I gingerly explored in my census blog, hesitant, at first, to handle the explosive topic of diversity.

No citizenship question appeared on the 2010 U.S. Census form, which was good because a lot of people wouldn't answer the EQ or the doorbell if they knew they'd be asked about citizenship. Speaking from experience, it's hard enough getting them to answer the questions without the citizenship issue smoldering on the back burner.

Census workers are diverse, but I didn't have the power to make it safe for someone to open the door and provide the information I sought. The best reassurance I could offer them was their PII data was legally protected from disclosure for 72 years, under U.S. Code Title 13. I wish it could feel safer and more comfortable for people of all races to answer the door and interact with the enumerator, but some are uncomfortable disclosing basic information about themselves.

The Census Bureau's 72-year confidentiality pledge also isn't enough to persuade everyone their data was private in this age of hacked websites.

No easy task, once a decade, census takers march forward with the nation's self-portrait, putting sharpened No. 2 pencils to forms and painting an immense block-by-block picture of who lives and sleeps in America.

REFUSAL

I slung the census bag on my back and trudged to my AA (Assignment Area). I'd run out of magic beans and used up all of my newcomer energy powering me through the first two weeks. I dreaded ringing the first doorbell.

I'd been trying to contact one household for a week; twice I'd left Form D-26, Notice of Visit, on the door. The windows were dark, but sounds of a baby and someone singing filtered out. I steadied the EQ and D1(F) Information Sheet atop my black binder, used as a writing surface, and rang the bell yet again.

The door opened, and a thin, pale young man with earlobe stretchers answered, his brown eyes soft. Smiling, I asked him to complete the

EQ, and when he hesitated, I handed him the Information Sheet and explained his answers were confidential for 72 years. I hoped he'd feel safe enough to cooperate–and then his Middle-Eastern-looking wife appeared behind him in the doorway, with a dark-eyed stare and a baby on her hip.

Her stubborn expression suggested she didn't trust me and wouldn't change her mind. Smoky incense poured out the door, and I flailed about for something to say to induce their participation. Inhaling the overwhelming smell of incense, I cleared my throat.

"The census figures are used for government funding for schools, day care centers, and nursing homes. They also determine the number of representatives in Congress," I said, my lips stretched over a tight smile.

"Can we refuse?" She cut me off in an accented voice.

"Well, if you—most people have been very cooperative." I coughed the incense out of my throat and glanced at the baby, perhaps for support, but the little guy fixed me with the same Medusa stare as his mother. We all sensed that what I was saying was not working.

"Is it optional, or a forced thing?" she asked, shifting him to the other hip. The technical answer is they could be fined or jailed for not answering the census, though it's rarely enforced.

"The decennial census is every ten years under the U.S. Constitution." I searched the young guy's face for a glimmer of hope and continued, "We live in a constitutional democracy…" His face soured, and I said, "Let's just answer the questions you want, and we can skip the rest."

Scanning the Information Sheet, he handed it back to me and murmured, "I need more information, and then I'll decide."

The wife piled on, sensing victory. "You want my social security number, don't you?" The incense tickled deep in my lungs, and I explained, no, we don't need social security numbers. I opened the EQ to show them the questions like a doctor going over x-rays with a patient.

Each person undercounted in the California Census costs the state more than $2,000 per year in federal funds. In 1990, California's population was undercounted in the census by 2.74 percent, resulting in the loss of $2 billion in federal funds over the next decade, along with the state's loss of one congressional seat. Census data collection has improved steadily over the decades, and the 2010 Census had an overcount of merely .01 percent, or 36,000 people— not statistically significant.

Historically undercounted groups include renters, immigrants, children, the homeless, and lesbian, gay, bisexual, and trans people. To avoid undercounting, California set aside $150 million for outreach to hard-to-reach populations in the recent 2020 Census, however the Trump administration's interference with the 2020

Census resulted in the worst undercount in decades: more on this later.

Resisting all my efforts, the couple backed into the house, and I let them go, persisting only so long as there was a prospect of completing even a partial EQ. I released my sneakered foot holding the door open, and it banged shut. Back on the sidewalk, I muttered to no one, "What is wrong with this block?" and spat an incense-flavored gob on the sidewalk.

The young family (Number in Household: 3) found themselves unable to cooperate with the census in a place where they could raise their son the way they wanted. I'll never know what fear drove the animosity in the wife's eyes. That is why a census citizenship question makes no sense. Nobody will answer truthfully; it's a "poison pill" dooming vital census questions to go unanswered; and it's no good conducting an inaccurate and incomplete count.

Americans demand the federal government protect us from enemies, disease, and unidentified white powder in the U.S. Mail, yet, for some, it's too much to divulge to the government our age, sex, and race during the census.

There's the homegrown paranoia of black helicopters and jack-booted government thugs, along with people of color fearing the police and immigrants worried about deportation. This is all wrapped up in the uniquely American mania for privacy, doorbell cameras, and surveillance, which only intensified by the time of the 2020 Census.

After all, why should any of us trust the government after Trump, Clinton, and Watergate? The political science major in me wants to trust what the government says and believe in our system of checks and balances. However, not everyone has faith in our government— even among those born here.

If you've never seen a cow, you don't know where milk comes from. And if you don't vote or participate in our democracy, you don't know where freedom comes from. The Constitution requires residents to fill out a form every ten years and mail it back, postage prepaid. The respondents contacted during NRFU ignored several notices from the Bureau, requiring a visit from the census worker, taking ten minutes of their time. It seems a small price, but not everyone's able to pay.

PROXY

After only four weeks of enumerating, my CL said the next week would be my last, and I could then slap INFO-COMMs, or memos, to the Bureau stating that a particular respondent eluded me, and abandon the chase. They wouldn't reappear like EQs had over the past weeks, returned to me to correct errors like not writing "No Middle Initial Person 2" in the margin, as I was trained to do.

A mere handful of grease-stained EQs remained, some of which had defeated three enumerators before me. The count was winding down, and that meant open season on proxies, neighbors who could provide relevant information in lieu of the unavailable respondent.

The steeplechase was on for proxy interviews for remaining respondents we hadn't yet contacted.

To close out the binders, I had to convey to the holdouts I wouldn't go away until they cooperated, and they could not evade the carpet bomb. I hit them by phone, doorbell, and through their landlord until they complied. Most landlords were cooperative but hard to track down.

Controversy swirled on another census blog about researching respondent information on internet sites like Spokeo. My CLA said it was okay to look up phone numbers on the Web, and afterwards backtracked, saying it wasn't approved by her superiors. A few days later, though, she said I could look up respondents' phone numbers on the internet — but the number got me nowhere if they didn't pick up the phone.

I met another enumerator returning from her shift. As we spoke, a car pulled in next to us, disgorging a mom, two kids, and a puppy. My fellow enumerator turned to me and said, "Proxy?"

I nodded. "I'll ask her."

But Supermom was too harried to help the census lady today.

Sometimes I cleaned up a block in one fell swoop, getting five proxies from one person. Often the block was deserted during the daytime, and I was lucky to get one EQ done. Many times, I tried to catch that last guy—the one who was never home, the one nobody knew anything about. "We all kind of keep to ourselves," said one man, when asked to be a proxy for his neighbor.

Ammonia cat box odor penetrated through the thick wooden front door of the woman with 16 cats (or 13, depending which neighbor I talked to) who didn't answer. Her next-door neighbor gladly gave a proxy interview in return for my sympathetic ear about the crazy cat lady next door.

All variables finally lined up to make census-by-bicycle possible for the first time; my new assigned area was a neighborhood that was too far to walk to, and the weather had warmed up. The bike's cargo rack made a handy work area.

That morning, my Lycra bike-shorted self plunked down a stack of blank EQs on the desk of a 20-something apartment manager in a business suit and heels. As I waited, she answered the phone and transferred the call, telling her co-worker who it was. After hanging up, she turned halfway towards me and said to the air, "What did I just say? What was the name I just said? I can't remember."

"I don't know, sorry," I said, impatient to get on with the interview. But as her eyes focused on me, she interrupted and said she had to leave, "So please hurry up."

"I don't like to be rushed," I said firmly, surprising myself.

"Well, I'm sorry," she said, "but I have to go somewhere in a minute, so you need to hurry."

I said, "Maybe your colleague could finish up if you have to go."

"No, I can finish it, just—let's go."

When we finished the EQs, I noticed the red betta fish in a sphere of yellow water on a credenza behind her desk. His bowl was the size of a large cantaloupe, and his fins sagged as he floated inside, watching the back of her head.

The next day my CL gave me another batch of mop-up EQs at the same apartment complex, where a different young manager pursed her lips and told me she had fifteen minutes to assist me.

"But there's thirty EQs here," I said, and we spent 45 minutes mining their tenant database for information to complete them.

On the credenza behind her resided a blue betta fish in an identical bowl, mirror image of the red betta in the other manager's office. I asked her, between questions about a tenant's sex and date of birth, "What's your fish's name?"

"Charlie," she replied in a little girl's high voice.

"Was it a gift?" I asked.

"Yes," she said, "because I saw the red betta in the other manager's office."

She gazed at me, Alice in Wonderland huge sapphire eyes, dark lashes, long straight hair, and I cleared my throat and returned to the questions. Charlie's bowl needed cleaning, fish turds covered the bottom. That evening, a Dr. Seuss rhyme popped into my head— *One Fish, Two Fish, Red Fish, Blue Fish*—and I went cross-eyed filling in the apartment manager's name on thirty forms with my yellow No. 2 pencil.

Unsurprisingly, the 2010 post-census evaluation found responses from proxy interviews to be less accurate than those given by a household member.

CENSORSHIP

The census smelled like old sushi, no longer fresh and exciting, but this enumerator was still counting, one dusty boot in front of the other, and blogging about it. Embedded with the troops, so to speak, I could not abandon my enumerator post, nor quit blogging about it, until it was well and truly done.

The "Confidentiality and Ethics Reminder" letter arrived inside my pay envelope from the Bureau, reminding us all not to reveal PII— Personal Identifiable Information. Around the same time, I noticed several other census blogs disappeared from the Web. I'd been careful not to reveal any PII on my blog, since they beat its sanctity into us during training.

Maybe other PII-leaking blogs prompted the Bureau to send up a warning flag after I'd posted several articles about the census on my own blog. The power of social media to threaten the security of PII, the beating heart of the census, sent civil servants scrambling to crank out a memo. Jeopardize PII, lose the public trust, and people won't participate.

The Bureau probably didn't care about my blog, even if it was on their radar, but I was angry. If I were shut down, I told my readers in a special update, I'd battle it with the help of the ACLU. My NRFU blog posts were my own impressions as an enumerator, boots on the ground with my shoulder bag and No. 2 pencils, and no one could take that from me, not even my employer, the U.S. government. I was certain the First Amendment protected my observations, opinions, and personal expressions from government interference.

And I made sure, even if I veered close to the line, there was no PII in my blog because I changed all the identities and personal details of respondents I wrote about. The characters were composites of my experiences as an enumerator—art, in other words.

My census blogging was not secret; I told my CL and CLA about it. Amongst the population of enumerators in 2010, bloggers and Tweeters were bound to emerge on social media, and our training failed to address the potential social media issues in advance, leaving the chips to fall where they may. Whether census operations are protected speech under Title 13 is a gray area, and the flyer gave the Bureau's narrow interpretation of the law.

I took what the Bureau gave me—the training, the shoulder bag, and the plastic pencil sharpener—and turned it into art, writing about refusals, dangers, practical considerations, and observations of human nature. Art cannot be censored in a democracy, not if it knows what's good for it. NRFU, for me, became a paid journalism internship, and I took the story and ran with it, like any good reporter.

The remaining census blogs, including mine, publicly accused the Bureau of censorship following the confidentiality notice and gave it another social media black eye. I doubt other bloggers revealed any PII—I know I didn't—but at least one other census blog closed up shop after the Bureau's notice, a cautionary tale about the government's ability to censor and chill free speech under the First Amendment.

Even if census bloggers didn't reveal PII, the confidentiality notice scared them away, which was perhaps the Bureau's intention. Maybe they got a few innocent bloggers shut down by implying they were in trouble for publishing census information.

In hindsight, it is clear the Bureau was not prepared to deal with the ramifications of the internet, with its blogs, tweets, and trolls, on the 2010 Census. Having learned its lesson, in 2020 the Census Bureau prepared an arsenal of tools to boost participation and combat misinformation and rumors. In addition to traditional media channels like billboards and radio, the 2020 Census created its own blogs, YouTube videos, email lists, and Twitter feeds to frame its message before social media got there first.

The census is a national "selfie" about who we are, what we look like, where we live and sleep, and with whom. I didn't want this job and thought I would suck at it, dreading every phase from training to interviews. My blog, which ten years later became this book, opened up the inner workings of the census and revealed what it's like to count Americans, my impressions of my country and its people, and how I changed during the course of NRFU.

In the end, the confidentiality notice gave me more material to blog about, since I had nearly finished my assigned binders and was running out of topics… or so I thought.

DOGTOWN

Once I finished the assigned blocks, I was asked to enumerate the area of West Oakland known as "Dogtown."

"Bad neighborhood, I'm telling you, it's a bad neighborhood," said my new Crew Leader, after Matt took a CPA job elsewhere.

I said, "I don't have any problem talking to anyone about anything. I'll say anything, within reason, to get them to fill out the EQ." I'd progressed a long way from my initial fear and reluctance to do interviews.

The first thing I noticed about the Dogtown EQs was they reeked of cigarette smoke. The trail had gone cold, the maximum six enumerator visits had been exhausted, and no interview. The enumerators still standing were the crackerjack team, hand-picked by our Crew Leaders for the Dogtown mission. The Field Operations Supervisor (FOS) called us "The Heavies" and commanded us to "get creative."

It was clear why previous enumerators didn't get the interviews: nobody wanted to be in Dogtown after 5 p.m., when people might be home. I pedaled past the Pak-n-Save shopping center and the freeway underpass spat me into a vintage neighborhood of low-slung former industry dependent on the nearby Port of Oakland, antique grain elevators, and modern storage facilities. Disused railroad tracks crisscrossed the pockmarked streets, entangling my bike wheels. Enumerating Dogtown by bicycle, I was level with the person with whom I was talking, yet could jet away quickly, squid-like, if I felt unsafe.

A parade of spindly-legged old men pedaled past me on bikes, towing garbage bins and shopping carts and balancing trash bags on their handlebars. For these bottle-and-can collectors, it was payday. The caravan rolled to the recycling center to exchange glass and metal for cash to buy alcohol or something to eat. There were hundreds of men and women collecting the recycling from residents' bins for money, and, like them, I had business in the neighborhood.

In this part of town white folks were rarely seen but, as always, my trusty shoulder bag and badge allowed me passage into worlds normally closed to me, to observe where folks live and sleep. To get anywhere with these residents, I would need to be—and not just appear—fearless. I sharpened my No. 2 pencil and left wood shavings on the sidewalk. My head was on a swivel, as Oakland streets had schooled me, looking behind me periodically to ensure no one was following, and noticing everything happening around me: cars, people, sounds, smells.

Immediately, I scored an easy interview. The person was home. My chat with the lady of the next house deteriorated as she stood on her porch, talking down to me. After evading a few questions, she barked, "I'm s'posed to believe you're a census worker because you have a nametag?" I decided to terminate the interview. "And get your bicycle off my property. It's basic courtesy!" she bellowed at my retreating back.

Along a wide boulevard, the front picture windows of mini-Victorians dozed along the once stately street, stagnant now with drugs, crime, and prostitution. Near the corner of Sav Mo Liquors and Pretty Woman Restaurant, I found the EQ address. I heard voices inside the house, but no answer. Pot-smoking men bunched on the sidewalk gave one-word answers while I got high on the secondhand smoke. *Fear is no good here*, I reminded myself.

Attracted by fluttering rainbow umbrellas, I chained my bike at the Rail Stop Deli, centered my government badge on my chest, and sauntered inside. "If I buy something, can I use the restroom?" I said.

"Yeah," the tiny Asian woman behind the counter said. She took ten minutes to make a customer's sandwich while I waited on one leg to ring up my soda and to be allowed to use the toilet. Later, I noticed she'd shortchanged me a nickel—to pay for the flush, I suppose. Ain't no free pee in Dogtown.

I got proxies from people hanging out who knew all their neighbors' business. Several street people provided information until I asked their name to write down on the form. They clammed up, and not impolitely loped away on inhumanly long basketball-player legs. "I gotta be somewhere," said one guy, sidling away from me and my inquiries.

Dogtown mesmerized me with its jacked-up sedans, scraper bikes, everybody knowing everybody, booming music from car windows, and marijuana in the air, cooking up a magic spell of everyday heat, poverty, and dust like a summer festival. Dogtown is like the Goodwill store, everybody knows everybody is poor, otherwise they'd be shopping—and living—somewhere better.

LAST SUPPER

The last weekend of May, I was among 30 enumerators and Crew Leaders chosen to meet with Odessa, the Regional Director who had trained and sworn us in. She asked us to spend the weekend enumerating in nearby Richmond, a city north of Oakland with a similar reputation for crime and poverty. After six weeks of enumerating, we were old hands now, and we received our binders for the weekend's Assignment Area. I was glad to have more enumerating to blog about, and the extra pay. Then a CL broke out plastic cups, snacks, and a bottle of cheap red wine, and I watched the Regional Director knock back a glass or two with the CLs.

It was a personal victory—I'd done well in my job, to break bread with the big kahunas like Jesus and his disciples at the Last Supper.

Almost like being promoted, we elite enumerators sipped wine and flipped through our new binders like fashion magazines. I didn't drink; I wanted to be sharp enumerating in Richmond the next day, jotting notes and blogging about it afterwards.

Each of us was assigned a partner. For the first time, we wouldn't work alone on this assignment. Mine was "Dave," a forty-something paunchy white guy who picked me up Saturday morning in a faded red Starsky-and-Hutch two-door sedan. He seemed genial enough, and off we roared 45 minutes north, like Special Forces parachuting in, with our binders and No. 2 pencils to pursue holdout respondents. I was relieved to hear Dave say he was a Crew Leader with "tons of experience."

His car, however, smelled of burning oil, which hurt my head. Our assignment was four blocks in South Richmond. I told Dave, "The neighborhood doesn't look that bad," as he jammed his tire into the curb outside the first address.

"Just because it's okay during the day doesn't mean it ain't bad at night," he grunted.

I crawled out of the jalopy and gulped in lungsful of fresh air, and before I knew what was happening, Dave strutted up the walk towards the respondent's front porch. I grabbed my binder and tottered along behind as he reached the threshold and hammered the door with his fist.

When a woman appeared, he stood spread-legged in front of her like a TV cop and barked, "U.S. Census, we'd like to ask you a few questions!"

"Nonono," I gasped, and rushed towards the door waving my arms so she wouldn't slam the door and ruin our last chance to reach her. As I ran forward, I realized his bragging about being an experienced Crew Leader must've been a lie—no enumerator would launch an interview in such an off-putting, aggressive manner.

Panting, I bounded up the steps with a disarming grin, apologized to the alarmed woman, and rescued the interview as Dave, his work done, scuffed back to the car and lit a cigarette. I was able to complete the Questionnaire, and, by unspoken agreement, he mostly played chauffeur the rest of the weekend, smoking in the car while I approached residences to ask the questions.

While driving, he blathered on his cell phone without a hands-free device, an illegal act in California. My suspicions grew when I saw sloppy errors on the few EQs he completed, but he frequently reminded me of his superior rank. Richmond didn't scare me half as much as Dave did. Where did they find him? And if he wasn't a CL, who was this impostor? I held my tongue and never did get satisfactory answers to my questions.

Each time I returned to the Starsky-mobile, it reeked of marijuana and burnt oil. He frequently got lost and had a bad habit of rolling down the car windows on both sides at red lights and shouting to the drivers on both sides, "Freeway? Where is Eighty, Eighty?" as if he weren't from the Bay Area, but visiting from Wisconsin.

It's only for two days, I reminded myself, frowning at his dented license plate sliding back and forth across the dashboard with every turn.

Safely home that night, redolent of pot and oil, I thought, *My census partner is not just a fraud, he's a burnout* (this was a decade before California legalized marijuana consumption). He was driving me around buzzed on the Government's dime. My safety was on the line, and I still had to enumerate with him the next day. It never occurred to me to ask for a different partner, because I needed the money and enumerating could end anytime. I wanted to make the most of any clean-up work I got, so I shut my mouth.

Our Sunday run was short, only three hours and six EQs, and I closed the vents on my side of the Starsky-mobile and opened the passenger window for fresh air.

Back in South Richmond, I craned my neck as we drove past a group of Black kids about twelve years old lugging heavy silver canisters of Roundup weed killer almost as big as they were around a church parking lot. In the Sunday sunshine, the kids pumped Roundup onto baby weeds growing in asphalt cracks. (An internet search later informed me that the Roundup label reads, "Keep Out of Reach of Children").

The boys wore khakis and matching jackets, while the girls were clad in frilly summer frocks with tight, shiny shoes. They obediently pumped chemicals from the sprayer hoses, likely drenching themselves in glyphosate, a human carcinogen. What had they done to deserve such punishment, community service, or simply abuse, those kids poisoning everything on the property, including themselves. Disturbed, I jotted down the scene to include in my blog.

That afternoon race was the subject of an argument I witnessed. The interview began with the mother who kept changing her answers as if she had dementia. Her grown son appeared, wearing a short blue velour bathrobe, and said, "Ask me the questions." Relieved, I continued the interview until Mom declared to her son that they weren't African American.

The son turned to her and said, "If you got black in yo ass, you Black—Black is all you is." They went back and forth while I tried to get in a word to finish the EQ. It was the 1970s sitcom "The Jeffersons" on acid. The son returned his attention to me and said, "I'm staying here after doing time for a crime that I committed."

The moment I decided to settle for half an EQ, my phone rang. It was my partner Dave calling, and I used the distraction to escape, never so glad to hear his testy voice. I could still hear them arguing through the screen door as we pulled away, and silently noted how the wording of the EQ questions on race practically guaranteed discord over ethnicity.

A few harrowing U-turns later, Dave delivered me to McDonald's for a bathroom break, where I came across fellow enumerators finishing paperwork. One thing he was right about, Richmond, like Oakland was a different town at night. One resident described his car being broken into three times, and his house three times, until he installed an iron fence with razor wire. Dave finally wheeled the Starsky-mobile towards home with two sets of bloodshot eyes behind the windshield.

The next day my phone rang.

Me: Hello?

Woman's Voice: Hello, this is the Census Office. Were you working in Richmond last weekend?

Me: Yes, I—didn't have any problems.

Voice: One of your respondents called here.

Me: Oh?

Voice: Yeah, she said that she was mean to you and wants to apologize.

Me (nearly dropping phone): Really?

Voice: She said that she didn't complete the EQ. She wants to do that by phone.

Me: Wow.

I remembered her gunning her PT Cruiser into the driveway as I left a Notice of Visit on her door. I strolled past her slowly, smiling and making sure to flash the embossed side of my shoulder bag. I greeted her from a respectful distance as she sat in her car, and she said, "I sent it in when I heard they were sending somebody to my house." Untrue, of course, but I kept smiling.

Standing in her driveway with my feet together, I bowed slightly, like a Chinese coolie from an old movie. She hadn't exited her vehicle, and I began to feel she wouldn't. I said, "You don't have to answer any questions you don't want to." The car door opened, and I saw a well-dressed, fit Black woman with a gray widow's peak.

"I'm busy, I have to put these groceries inside and leave after that," she said as I fell casually into step beside her. "That's okay, I can do this while you do that," I said, and asked the questions while she unloaded her bags.

"My age!" she cried. "Sixty-one." And I saw she instantly regretted telling me. After that, she would not answer further, got back in the car and pulled out, with me waving in her rear-view mirror. I had a slight glow of satisfaction that I never lost my cool, whereas she lost her temper. I had to snatch small victories where I could from the jaws of defeat.

When I returned her call, she said she'd had a death in the family and apologized for her behavior. Richmond was supposed to be a hard case, but it produced the only apology I received as an enumerator. She also commended me on my professionalism; she wasn't about to let me win the politeness contest.

The job was like stand-up comedy—you're either on fire or you're dead.

VACANT DELETE

Finally, there was light at the end of the trench. NRFU would end for us on June 10. We had until then to finish our binders, complete INFO-COMMs, get proxies for refusals, and close NRFU. My CL said there were other census-related jobs beyond NRFU, so maybe I'd get more work to blog about.

When enumerating ended, I recalled where I started—it seemed longer than three months—dreading every second, hating the door-to-door aspect, ashamed of the job. Enumerating turned all my expectations on their head. The respondents were pleasantly helpful, for the most part, gracious, and helped me to garner pride in myself, my country and the work.

My mistakes became learning opportunities, allowing me to see myself as gutsy, a valuable asset to my employer and society. I showed bravery, persistence, and resourcefulness in tracking people down and getting EQs done. And I ended up, by all accounts, a successful enumerator, even tapped to crack the "hard nut" of South Richmond.

Burned into my mind were the blocks I had enumerated, where I had refusals, proxies, hidden units, small wins. I thought enumerator was an easy job to get, the test was cinchy—until I met wannabe enumerators who were on their third or fourth try to pass the exam. I never doubted the dedication of the enumerators and Crew Leaders, though I had, at times, doubted their sanity, along with my own. Nevertheless, I experienced newfound confidence and emotional and financial stability from enumerating.

Three times the Bureau called me to work on vacant-delete, after I complained publicly on my blog over not being selected. Yet I refused, having already secured a new temporary job as a Union Organizer, which used the same skill set as enumerating. I answered an ad, interviewed, and became part of a team of people working in hospitals and college campuses convincing employees to sign cards demanding the right to unionize. The pay was about the same as enumerating, however I worked mostly in teams, not alone as I had when enumerating.

The Union job lasted a good two months, and then I again faced unemployment.

Walking to the store in mid-June, I observed a young man juggling enormous black binders on the corner—an enumerator!—with a mixture of nostalgia and amusement. I hurried up and flashed my shoulder bag at him, now used as a shopping tote, to indicate that I was a fellow census taker.

"Hi," I said. "Doing Vacant-Delete?"

"I'm done," he said.

"Already? I thought they were training this week."

"The training was last week."

We continued across the street at the walk signal.

"Done already?" I said with a grin.

Shifting the load to his other arm, he said, "I'm with the Coast Guard Reserve. I'm going to the Gulf of Mexico to help with the Deepwater Horizon oil spill."

"Really! How do you feel about that?"

"It's an environmental disaster," he said, and I noticed the wedding band on his left hand.

"Apocalypse," I agreed. "Don't breathe the oil, whatever you do." He chuckled, but I continued, "It'll make you sick. Wear a respirator, even if they tell you not to."

We reached the train station, and he stopped and held out his hand. "Ted," he said. I shook it. "Take care," he said.

"You too," I said as he faded into the platform rush-hour throng. Watching Ted with his binders, I felt relief to no longer be enumerating. I wished my fellow enumerator well in oil gusher hell, and felt proud of him at that moment. And proud of myself for being part of the 2010 Census team.

DR. GROVES

Weeks after NRFU ended, I discovered the online blog of Dr. Groves, the national Census Director, and its trove of information. He praised the enumerators—the "ground troops of the largest civilian operation in the U.S." He wrote he had spent a few weeks traveling with enumerators on their rounds. I pictured him waiting in the car puffing on a pipe, watching the enumerator wrangle the interviewee on the porch.

Groves raised his binoculars in a wreath of smoke like a British safari guide, observing the enumerator-respondent interaction, and, as he wrote, "Good enumerators try to link the life concerns of the residents to the benefits of the census, but often they have only seconds to do so before the door closes." It crossed my mind the good doctor had, indeed, been reading my census blog posts all along.

These were his parting words to the enumerators:

You were among the best labor force for a decennial census in decades; you brought to the census family the strongest set of skills and intelligence, the best work experience, incredible flexibility, and a strong devotion to serving the American public by devoting your talents to the 2010 Census. On behalf of the full Census Bureau family, I thank you for your service to the country, and I wish you well in the next steps in your careers. I hope some of the experiences you had during this massive, complicated, messy effort will provide knowledge that makes you a better employee in your next endeavor.

Although we were apparently one big happy census family, a torrent of negative comments followed his post, detailing unpaid wages and constant rule changes. I was grateful not to have had those problems while working on the census. A fellow named Jeff said, "This job is not for the faint of heart." Amen, brother.

Dr. Groves again credited the census workers for a successful NRFU in his blog post of August 10, 2010:

16. DR. GROVES

The temporary census workers we hired, in this time of high unemployment rates, were just spectacular. They put in the hours; they worked more efficiently than we were expecting; they made our field processes go smoothly.

In December, Commerce Secretary Gary Locke announced that the 2010 Census came in $1.87 million under budget. Unlike Dr. Groves, he credited "strong management" that overcame criticism of the census as wasteful and inefficient.

According to the census mission to "count everyone once, only once, and in the right place," the 2010 count was highly accurate, with an estimated overcount of .01 percent, or 36,000 extra residents counted out of an overall U.S. population of 330 million.

From NRFU, I learned how to encounter someone on the street and ask for personal information. How to saunter through unfamiliar, confusing, or dangerous neighborhoods without fear. How to say the right thing in an effort to stop the door from slamming in my face. To hold my tongue when someone kicks me out of their yard until I'm off the property (then curse them out of earshot). I can scratch out the smallest patch of common ground with someone totally unlike me, and sharpen my No. 2 pencil on the fly.

FURTHUR

When interviewing an elderly respondent, I often wondered if he'd make it to the 2020 decennial census. And what about myself—would any of us be around in ten years? The answer in my case is I am still here, by the grace of God.

In many ways, I'm still recovering financially from the "Not-So-Great Recession." It turns out the federal government taxed those unemployment benefits that saved me from destitution, so I wound up with a whopping tax bill I couldn't pay. Once the census series ended, my blog readership declined, and the next year I stopped blogging. Maybe these things have a natural cycle. My census series was an unexpected hit, and now it's become the book you're reading.

In 2013, I began working for a company started in 2008 that pairs "Taskers" with customers needing work done on an app platform. I found success in the variety of temporary work I could get there, including house cleaning and organizing. After four years of "tasking," I struck out on my own with my house cleaning business, which has been fun, though I'm still not making enough money to repay my law school loans.

A former lawyer cleaning houses? Yes—underemployment is a continuing legacy of the Great Recession, for me, if not for other Americans. I actually enjoy cleaning and organizing much of the time, and my clients are the best. But there are those days, scrubbing my third toilet, when I wonder what the hell I'm doing with my life, when I could be earning more and working a less strenuous job. I haven't forgotten the lessons I learned during the census and the "Not-So-Great Recession."

The neighborhoods I enumerated became familiar as old friends to me, and navigating around town I'll say to myself with an inner smile, "I took the census here."

2020 CENSUS INNOVATIONS

Citizenship and Politics

In 2017, the Department of Justice under President Donald Trump asked the Census Bureau to add a citizenship question to the census, a request guaranteed to stir controversy. A citizenship question last appeared on the census form in 1950, and since 2005, the citizenship query has appeared only on the American Community Survey, which goes to 3.5 million households annually.

In June 2019, the Supreme Court decided in *Department of Commerce v New York* that the Constitution requires all people to be counted, regardless of whether they are citizens, can vote, were born here or elsewhere. This protects against manipulation of the number of U.S. House Representatives, and ensures that undercounted communities are not shortchanged of federal funding allocation based on the census.

The Census Bureau estimated that including a citizenship question would reduce census responses among households with one or more noncitizen by at least 8 percentage points. Had the Supreme Court not blocked the citizenship question, it would have exacerbated the undercount in communities of color.

Trump's census micromanaging and delays prompted Bureau Director Robert Santos, President Biden's appointee, to declare that the census was "being sabotaged" to benefit Republicans.

Technology and Accuracy

In an effort to lower costs and increase participation, the census questionnaire was available online, a first, raising concerns about cybersecurity, as well as U.S. residents who don't have reliable access to the internet.

And, for the first time, NRFU numerators didn't rely on paper and pencil in 2020, as each one was issued a dedicated Apple iPhone 8 loaded with a newly-developed census app using security measures like two-factor authentication. The app was designed to function without network connectivity, given the varied field locations where enumerators operate.

About two-thirds of U.S. households answered the 2020 Census online, however the rate of unanswered census questions was the most ever: a record 10% to 20% of questions were left blank. Experts feared the Trump administration's failed threats to add a citizenship question and to end the census count early depressed the response rate.

Enumerators were trained in social distancing due to the COVID-19 pandemic and subsequent lockdown that struck just as census materials were mailed out. The pandemic negatively affected the data collection, as well.

In contrast to the 2010 count, as the Census Bureau reported in May 2022, the 2020 Census undercounted minority groups, and the error was highest for Black people (3.3%) and Latinos (5%). It also missed 4.8% of children under 5.

Following the release of census results in 2021, California and New York both lost a seat in the House of Representatives, while several other states like Texas gained congressional seats for the next ten years.

Despite fourteen states being miscounted in 2020, the Bureau declared the results "fit to use" to assign the states' congressional seats, Electoral College votes, and to redraw voting districts. The follow-up report confirmed that the incorrect count wouldn't change those delegations.

Trust and Safety Team

In December 2019, the Census Bureau announced the establishment of a new "Trust and Safety Team" to combat "misinformation and disinformation" about the census so that everyone had the facts and felt safe responding to the 2020 Census. "If people get the wrong information about the Census—intentionally or unintentionally—it poses a problem for all of us," said the press release.

The Trust and Safety Team "monitored all channels and platforms in traditional media and social media for misinformation and disinformation about the census," and responded to rumors and "urban legends," which is a pretty fair description of my own census blog in 2010.

The 2020 Census expected to deal with "scammers, criminals, fraudsters, trolls, unscrupulous opportunists, and malicious actors." In addition, "friendly supporters of the census and well-meaning groups can accidentally spread misinformation when the information they have is incorrect."

Though well-meaning, Trust and Safety Team monitoring could be overbroad and have a chilling effect on free speech about the 2020 and future censuses. Just as the cautionary letter about confidentiality had the possible effect of closing down some census blogs in 2010, overzealous protectionism of future censuses may discourage journalists, bloggers, Tweeters, and podcasts from honest, in-depth reporting, especially if the Bureau itself made an error. I question whether my freewheeling, opinionated 2010 Census blog would've survived scrutiny by this "truth squad."

No doubt, the Trust and Safety Team will eventually get its hands on this book to determine if it contains misinformation or urban legends about the census. (Spoiler alert: it does!) Perhaps the Team will go through my firsthand observations, experiences, and impressions of the census with a fine-toothed comb—a thrilling prospect. However, since this book is about the 2010 Census, it is no threat to the smooth functioning of censuses to come.

Outreach

With the 2020 Census, the Bureau was eager to get out in front and make use of the internet and social media, from hackathons to educational YouTube videos and webinars, with an emphasis on multicultural strategies to encourage participation of historically undercounted minority groups.

The 2010 Census was conducted as if the internet and social media didn't exist, from its outreach campaign all the way down to the pencil-and-paper data collection method. Instead of the internet, the census employed a truck convoy, even a census-themed race car to publicize the census and encourage Americans to respond to the questionnaire. The Bureau was caught flat-footed, confronted by social media bloggers like me, the DIY journalists who filled the vacuum.

GLOSSARY OF CENSUS ACRONYMS AND WORDS

Apartment Mix-up Exactly what it sounds like.

Census Day The reference day of April 1, every ten years during the **Decennial Census** The date when all U.S. residents' addresses are recorded. It has been suggested that Census Day be a national holiday.

Crew Leader (CL) Person who supervises a team of census enumerators during **Nonresponse FollowUp (NRFU)** in the field. **Crew Leader Assistant (CLA)** is the deputy assisting the **Crew Leader.**

D-547 and D-590 Enumerator Training Manuals The reference books given to **Enumerators** during their Training Week, containing policies and procedures learned during the training.

Decennial Census The every-ten-years population count conducted by the U.S. Census Bureau under the U.S. Department of Commerce, mandated by Article I of the United States Constitution.

Enumerator A Census Bureau employee who interviews people in-person to complete EQs (Enumerator Questionnaires) of households not responding by mail to the mailed Questionnaire, during **NRFU**.

Enumerator Questionnaire (EQ) The census form filled out by **Enumerators** interviewing respondents in person, when following up with nonresponding households.

Field Operations Supervisor (FOS) Supervises a group of CLs and census takers to monitor performance and ensure the quality of work is maintained.

INFO-COMM Census Form D-225, Information Communication to the Dept of Commerce; a memo the Enumerator fills in to transmit information about an issue, like a respondent refusal to cooperate, a payroll problem, or an apartment mix-up.

In-Movers Respondents who move into their current residence after April 1 of the census year (See **Census Day**, above).

Local Census Office (LCO) The temporary local office headquarters for **Enumerator** teams, indicated by a four-digit number.

Nonresponse Followup (NRFU) When teams of **Enumerators** go door-to-door, tracking down people who didn't respond to the census form they received by mail, to interview them and fill out the form.

Personally Identifiable Information (PII) Data such as name, address, or date of birth that can be used to identify an individual **Respondent,** which **Enumerators** are sworn to protect for 72 years.

Proxy Interview Neighbors, landlords, and apartment managers who provide information about residents who cannot be located by **Enumerators** during **NRFU.**

Respondent An individual resident who fills out the census questionnaire or provides answers to the questions on the **Enumerator Questionnaire (EQ)** during **NRFU.**

U.S. Census Bureau A division of the U.S. Department of Commerce in charge of collecting and disseminating statistics about U.S. people and economy.

Writing Conventions Instructions for **Enumerators** to write letters and numbers as shown, for example: "When printing an M or N, DO NOT ROUND THE HUMPS." (D-547 Enumerator Manual)

ACKNOWLEDGEMENTS

Thank you to my beta readers, everyone who supported and encouraged me, and to all those who fostered in me a love of books.

ABOUT THE AUTHOR

Annalee Cobbett writes and cleans in Northern California with a cat or two, and this is her first book. She graduated cum laude from Mary Washington College, and earned a Juris Doctorate from the University of Richmond.

www.ingramcontent.com/pod-product-compliance
Lightning Source LLC
Chambersburg PA
CBHW032146040426
42449CB00005B/418